MW00966359

christmas 2008

To Kelsey

From Grandma and Poppey

You Are God's Gift to Me

CHRIS SHEA

THOMAS NELSON
Since 1798

NASHVILLE   DALLAS   MEXICO CITY   RIO DE JANEIRO   BEIJING

Published in Nashville, Tennessee, by Thomas Nelson. Thomas Nelson is a registered trademark of Thomas Nelson, Inc.

Cover design by Robin Black, Blackbird Creative.

Thomas Nelson, Inc., titles may be purchased in bulk for educational, business, fund-raising, or sales promotional use. For information, please e-mail SpecialMarkets@ThomasNelson.com.

ISBN: 978-1-4003-1411-9

www.thomasnelson.com

Printed and bound in China.

For Steve
My friend, my gift.

Every good gift
and every perfect
gift
is from above
and comes
down
from the Father
of
lights.
James 1:17

There is a wonderful
array of
gifts
in the world.

clocks and dolls,
toasters,
Pearls,
watches and
bikes, goldfish
and
beautiful
bouquets
of
flowers.

But the best gift
I can think
of

is you,

you,
whose heart
is
tender

and
Kind,

whose
smile
I
cherish
more

than the costliest
work of art.

You are
a gift
God
sent
to
me,

love,
God

a
happy blessing,
an
answered
prayer.

Of
this
I
have no
doubt.

Because nothing but God's amazing grace

could account for the
joy of you
in my life.

Only the Father
of
lights
could send
such a treasure
as
You.

where could you
come from, but the heart
of the One who is Love?

If only the
words existed
that would express
all you mean
to me...

...but no such words
have been
invented.

You add joy
to my
life,

It's true!

and color to

my

World ,

you
really
do!

And

sometimes
just the
thought of you

makes me so happy I could cry.

Yours is the face...

... I can't
wait
to
see .

Yours is the laugh...

... I love to hear.

When the world feels cold,

thoughts of you make
it warmer.

And
When a day feels dark,

the sight of you makes it
brighter.

The One,

who sent

starlight

and

fireflies...

...sent
you
as well.

Planets!
Butterflies!
The moon shining
     high in
       the
         sky!
           You!...

All sent from
God and wrapped
up in His
Love.

Love,
God

(I happen
to think,

you were one
of
God's best
ideas ....)

You lift me up

when I'm feeling down,

and make me
laugh

when I'm
feeling blue;

When I'm with you,
I wish I could
keep the
sun from
setting...

so the
day
would
never
end.

Not a day goes
by,

not a single one

Thank you
Thank you
Thank you.

that I don't give
God thanks...

for your dear heart,
your sweet face,
the sound of your
voice

and
your knock on
my door.

I thank Him
for the
good gift,
the perfect
gift,
sent from
up
above ...

I thank Him
for
the
gift
of

you!